CONSTRICTOR

CONSTRICTOR

Nathaniel G. Moore

Mansfield Press

Library and Archives Canada Cataloguing in Publication

Title: Constrictor / Nathaniel G. Moore.
Names: Moore, Nathaniel G., author.
Description: Poems.
Identifiers: Canadiana 20210340398 | ISBN 9781771262781 (softcover)
Classification: LCC PS8626.O595 C66 2021 | DDC C811/.6—dc23

Editor for the Press: Jim Johnstone
Cover Design: Erica Smith
Author Photo: Amber McMillan
Typesetting: Denis De Klerck

The publication of *Constrictor* has been generously supported by the Canada Council for the Arts and the Ontario Arts Council.

ONTARIO ARTS COUNCIL
CONSEIL DES ARTS DE L'ONTARIO
an Ontario government agency
un organisme du gouvernement de l'Ontario

Canada Council for the Arts
Conseil des arts du Canada

Mansfield Press Inc.
25 Mansfield Avenue, Toronto, Ontario, Canada M6J 2A9
Publisher: Denis De Klerck
www.mansfieldpress.net

for

Thomas Carl Norden

1973-2020

Katie Lameck

1975-2015

TABLE OF CONTENTS

PROPER CONCERN 9

KAFKA TEARS 11
WE'LL LET YOU KNOW 12
QUALICUM BEACH 14
CONSUMER BOULEVARD 16
MY WAY HOME, THE DOG IS LONG 19
DOWNTOWN 20
FROGMEN, 1995 21
RICHARD 22
SUSSEX POSTCARD 24
SCARLET TO PLAY FLUORESCENT NIGHTINGALE 25
TACET NOX 26
THE RABBIT 27
THERE ARE ANTS IN THE CARPET 28
DUCKWORTH'S POOL IN NORTH LEASIDE 29
DAVID LEE ROTH CHARLES BUKOWSKI FREE REFILLS 30
PARKLIFE 31
'SILVERBLADE' NOVELIST MARGARET ATWOOD 34

SULPICIA'S SCHOOL FOR BAD GIRLS 35

GEMINUS VEXILLUM 37
SULPICIA'S ROMAN GRANDMOTHER 41
KATHY ACKER RIDES THE BUS 42
SULPICIA'S BREAKFAST FEEDBACK 43
JUNKYARD BEACH HOME 44

CONSTRICTOR 45

NOTES 68
ACKNOWLEDGEMENTS 69

PROPER CONCERN

KAFKA TEARS

1.

I set my self a goal today
in a haze, a loquacious maze
I will not die nor will I decay
my sites no longer set on stun,
the night betrays

2.

some great things in the world
two dogs asleep on the couch rain slackened
I am fine don't you worry bout me bay-beeeeeeeeee
Elvira in make up kissing me, such a ghoul
the guns have melted the stables unglued
it was organic it was full of bliss
I run panting from the fields of betrayal
the night is razoring I am the night

3.

I offer God a solid image to console
then say stiffly, I don't know if I love
you girl, I just know—
rust coloured sticky phlegm,
sharp stabbing pain sinks
deeper with each breath
—I have pneumonia
fever rips the appetite plunges
she won't go away from me
  I've got Kafka lungs here
I can't come home dear
the night is red I am the night

WE'LL LET YOU KNOW

A bicarbonate of soda in the eyes? Eyes? Sure.
Two or six flaming pinwheels of beauty face
to face with a bat I can't fly sepia street lights
spelling out FELINE and don't forget the plastic
lawn furniture, a circus of terrific dandelions,
an old shudder with a paint blue Pac-Man
ghost while the ugly brick coloured slate
siding along the garage makes up fifteen point
eight per cent of our view metal fire pit converted
into a feeder of birds, eater of worlds;
two apple trees dusted in OFF bug spray
the brand of family mutations, you know,
Uncle Kafka an empty tin can punctured
with holes on its way to lantern sunset
summer borders frost I am describing our backyard
in the poem's present tense with *Hints of 1994*, asterisks

as if to suggest *Hints of 1994* is a proper name
it's just three words in a poem, cruel, the only pining
clawing at the notion of a single year's cruelty as vintage,
needling numb towards the surface as we see a present
tense pine tree branch get chewed by downtown dogs
and a rusty circular grill resting on fence a child's club
house repurposed for firewood storage solar powered
lights wrapped warpily trees sutures on a limb in the light
of day vulnerable in a moment of calm observation
as I try to disengage myself from the oversaturated glucose
charged realisms my own sense of...oh the glory of it all
why did I think I could do *this* then?

I was twenty I was listening to music so was Sarah
the bulimic high school senior, terror-eyed
no contact 1990s pal my stigmatic my pills
my psychiatric trickles anxious behaviour
bedeviled Christ like wounds and smoke rings
  "Deb hates it when we smoke in here, well,
her mom does."

"Is a Sally Ann (Salvation Army) minister capable of hate?"
our break up occurred in between reading *Adventures in the*
Skin Trade, while my amateur hour of written words mailed
to her acted out a jealous teleplay guaranteed anti-foreplay
a sort of syndicated lover's quarrel, easy to discard

"Debra look!" Sarah shouted, lowering the blanket
revealing two or three breasts, and Debra continued
her exit, "I've already seen your knockers Sarah,"
a helluva time and you know, I didn't age for three months
straight—hair didn't grow, stomach didn't growl

at our uptown here-you-go-loser-poet on Mount Pleasant
near uptight Eglinton[1] when Sarah handed me my maligned
notebook, its yellow cover with index tabs, handed over
unenthusiastic, fantastic muse drop out I was a living teenage
wreck aged to self-defection.

Do you know, just for fun, a bottle of 1994 Marilyn Monroe
Wines 'Marilyn' Merlot from Napa Valley California costs
$94.56 so let's toast to the possibilities

---

[1]It was sunny early 1995 and she handed me my coiled notebook as I fell deeper into a Babylonian brook nearly drowning – my poems were in her position for one hundred days, vulnerably arranged ready for disdain zero courage

QUALICUM BEACH

Empty your mind of the rush water floods fix,
no switch out that old orange door which hits
hard against each wave on top of it
with confidence, lay long ways—we never
should have tried to build a house on water
in the ocean real estate realism
never our strongest stroke breach the first wave—
as it crests our own private mad beach rich
with sodium sandy knees
the waves are greater still moving thrashing
a culmination of death we took a ride
with our hammer, our level and plane
in the riptide for a half century
we returned by dusk one evening standing up
her voice soft and close; a castle drawbridge
firmly open

to her body the ocean felt like molded plastic
cold while the whitecaps proved nothing more
than a foamy afterthought above the ocean's
wild curves seven photographers swarm
the spot where she once sat pyretic dreaming
of old songs, staring at bedroom wall dents
from yearbook hissy fits, skipping
over the gloom deluge of faces snarling
like a one-way mirror
makes you feel criminal, a blight on the glass,
as each face sticks funeral-ready eyes sandy yes
tingling skin no more someone hears her in
quarantine in need of another voice a warmth
of amphetamines colours her dulls dampens
donuts christening a beach with laughter
she dream kissed the morning on the neck
an open face sculpted in eros

last time corrupted by wet memory an oily
portrait hinting at her to sleep dead sun set
in her back pocket polluted space between speech
silence bodies warmed by windowsill sun milking

CONSUMER BOULEVARD

for Warren

When I was a young lad
corporate icons made me glad
saw the way they taught me things
recognized them bootprints
in the hall
    "Draw not this night, take off your shoes,
make no more artwork," mother said to me,
I have a song to sing to you son

So she sang, "so many things resemble
products out on the street"
    I may have nodded, watching her
shimmy in her famous bloodred apron
a gray guitar slung over her shoulder,
a dusty rolling pin
   in her left hand,
"Son, listen, I find it hard son, I find it weird,
how products compete with my need
    for a sense of well-being and
adjustment"
    she began to strum in a most
beautiful way
   I couldn't fret I listened well
as she sang of fiber optics, Tabasco
and her time on the boulevard
of enhancement, how
one day I too would walk along
    its generous offerings,
how it would "helps my glands"
what is a consumer? I asked, and she kept
on singing as my homework grew cold

When my mother died I sang her song
as best I could remember
  a song of sustenance,
of fractured realism, of domestic
bliss, culinary deception,
endless scabs never healing
  invisibly plucked
despite always giving Jesus
  his weekly stipend

lines I sang the loudest:

she walked down Consumer Boulevard
far too many times, thinking how she'd like to invest
some time in her own stable economy

mourners twisted began to sway
mourners listening held up rolling pins
    faces daubed in Holy flour

to end I sang in a voice
of forced grit, sandpaperistic

mother sharpened her last dagger
threw it through the wall
I knew I couldn't eat
off the crack in the wall

sawdust made out of the dead
I saw drywall instead of lead

smartbomb love letters
mother always had money for stamps

she was kind she must have thought:
I will be thy mouth and I will be thy tongue

MY WAY HOME, THE DOG IS LONG

for Tavis

But mostly I miss your half-lit eyes
yellow playful in the dog park

of our weeknight weakness
elastic wind panting as we locked horns

you see, my way home, the dog is long
describe to me again the make believe

contents of your Polish elbow a gorgeous
bone, you said a fairy lives, giving you

advice because I can't remember
no matter how often the doctor spikes

my rancid paper cup. Everyone said it
was September everyone thought

of leaves everyone smelled old exhaust
please stop this nostalgic glitch

faces moist in gray night sleep in green
sweaters in charcoal afternoons

with nervous cigarette whispers
our heads leaning up against a dying

oak tree after. A passing feeling red orange
harvestial nature footage unalterable each

song we heard the lyric ironic, plagued with woo-hoo
youth falling into sturdy oak tree not dying at all kissing

DOWNTOWN

I never knew that I could be in love like this crisp
yellow cotton broadcloth. Bishop collar; buttons in

the back. Machine washable. Belted skirt: green
textured fabric of Fortrel polyester cotton. Hip

stitched front pleats; back zipper *with just one kiss*
look what has happened I am always walking

somewhere with these knees with grocery ghosts
hidden by parcels lassoed by squirrel tails,

car exhaust ghosts by I see them run I see them go
green and lay flat on the grass

I don't know what makes me love you so much
I only know I never want to let you go ever since

today I'll go to the park I'll read *The Power of Positive*
Thinking I'm not going to be sick today. Now, listen honey,

I fell into your open arms I didn't stand a chance
when you're alone life loans you a lonely downtown

when worries hurry you may find some body lifeless
on the sidewalk how can you move? Everything sways

in a coral reef of static, a gentle bossa nova never
closes before the night is slivered in happiness

the lights are much brighter just like me, my name
is Kathy yes, with a gentleman's hand in love

FROGMEN, 1995

One frozen morning Ontario's Lost Boys dissolved
voice shards shoreline *No, nothing yet* no one no
sees saw clothing no shoes no socks left or right
no belt no hat – woolen, cotton-poly blend baseball no
Yankees Jays Red Sox belonging to Chad Smith
Danny Higgins Jay Boyle Jamie Lefebvre
Michael Cummins Robbie Rumboldt
four witnesses suggest a stolen Boston Whaler
a four-metre imitation motorboat "goof around" on
Frenchman's Bay stolen ghosting across lake Ontario
boys o boys capsized in hypothermia aching cold
gasping gripped boys within minutes massive
search Sunday start Durham police Toronto police
marine unit, Hercules C-130 aircraft, marinating
in proper concern, propeller twirling from air-sea
rescue unit found nothing thousands across southern
Ontario joined hunt no bodies no boats no pieces of
clothing found only a gas can from Boston Whaler
many eyes on Lake Ontario filled with broken, glassy
minutes of icy trauma of icy ruin lost one very early
very morning hours we think they stole two boats
for a joyride no one really knows how to say goodbye

RICHARD

I'm rotten on your love, and will die
from the red when you have finally waved
the flag. I love you in the brutal truths of this storm.
I can't store this liquor anymore, this evaporating heart
with these possessed poetics, I began to write
you dirty, I began the quest I lick the thumbprints
from your face never clean never there.

Your love is tinsel, the snap is oh so near
New Year's garbage I accept the terms of God
you enter a mirror house
nearing the edge now, before dark blankets
your plump ass cannot break the frame,
I juggle hope and phantom words, I simmer
the fat from bone *when you are wild*
in the forest, when you wear
a necklace of nothing lust.

Bill Gates has compromised things, too.
His messaging software has led you from my idea
of Wednesday night, I've been recording this pain lust
as love invincible, ballads shadowbox in my throat
not invisible, not a fragment or reduced bravery,
my sweat teems from limbs; I am jealous of words
slung in the night. I'm jealous of feverless sleep.
You shed/I shed tears and pounds,
I shed words from the bricks of my book.
What will we call you? Sacrifice? At least you
had space with me, it was a natural moment
when our hands touched. It's already been acted out online,
so many times, fulfilling some edgy ritual monitored
by dial-up satellite guiding your drizzling,
lowercase, pink ribbon tantrums; a light
that never goes out. There is a love still waiting.

The ocean was ours first because there your blood
mixed with salt, there your body learned to crawl,
where our tongues played with God, jaw-dropping
shadows punctured harsh, and all that remained
was the light. And our eyes, dancing into the heat.

SUSSEX POSTCARD

Kite in lilting sun you tether the sky
sky a fractured font

font from an endangered postcard
postcard curdled from years of neglect

neglect you get lonely wanton
wanton as you stride in a tattered apron

apron exaggerated like athlete renewed ambition
ambition for campfire singe along interventions

interventions unwanted, not wanton, cull your jets
jets eek out a finality against sedative rock

rock lulls a boy, a baby boy in the tree taupe
taupe sky brightens as wino finds Jesus sleeping

sleeping one off in a pamphlet centrefold discrete
discrete crushes a chemical imbalance

imbalance, your head held high, like a kite

SCARLET TO PLAY FLUORESCENT NIGHTINGALE

Yo Joe tease the hair again while hard-on beneath denim
un vrai briseur de cœur comic book page stopper, crossbow

heart breaker in a bathrobe her inky buns sitting shotgun
she snaps, "We could be killed up ahead. Excuse me while

I change into my fighting clothes." Scarlet is drawn tight,
a peacekeeper, a dominatrix, a red-headed superkiller

Scarlet dreamed of magical horses running Panasonically
through trances in soft fields forever Energizeresque

your sudden touch along my knee-skinned truths
is an agony in an ecstasy liked toys Duracellian

my friends each holding a wet piece of poly-cotton from
my ripped Tinker shirt. "And you keep your eyes on the road."

TACET NOX

Sitting at the Plutonium Bluffs Library
just outside of Nanaimo
staff room kettle boils
  to a vapour
shame about them off-putting
December hours
while ten miserable acerbic
ghosts cry out,
dehyrdrated, unemployed,
raging with me
where seventy dainty slaves
began to chew
the non-fiction walls
with crocodile implants
tacet nox
talcum night
janitor night, Santa in a toga
where is Jesus et les trois reines?
Hey Romulus, wing these antelopic
farm things from our memory,
lest the birds ascend again
all fees waved

THE RABBIT

Make the narrative arc out of two
by fours cease your concomitant whining
the carbs are in the bloodstream the dogs
and children are napping
your house is talking to you again
not surprisingly you are talking back
I am a thing who sees forks
on the ground but often ignores
their cold position along the dirt floor
I know of a town where drawers exist,
I'll see that fork again this afternoon
the snow a tablecloth lit by a greasy skyline
the hare moves towards the stick and basket

THERE ARE ANTS IN THE CARPET

I bought him a few bottles of beer I found the ice machine
I stuck to my generous pours of rum and Coke acidic Reaganomics
blood flow childhood death all of us a bleed in the print run
I bought him a few bottles and found the ice machine outside
I was sticking to my generous pours of rum and Coke the acidic
I bought him a few bottles of beer I found the ice machine
I stuck to my generous pours of rum and Coke acidic Reaganomics
blood flow childhood death blood flow a fingerprint on the lens
newspaper photographs washed out a face hollownarrowvacant
clean the tableau from which to walk away, past a boy cutting open
a bundle of afternoon newspapers in a tavern silent hours evaporate
I bought him a few bottles of beer I found the ice machine
I stuck to my generous pours of rum and Coke acidic Reaganomics
blood flow childhood death the paperboy delivered the ghostly news

DUCKWORTH'S POOL IN NORTH LEASIDE

You swam like a swan free of worry free of fat rolls distinguished
by chlorine pool collaged in real time with your long sleeved t-shirt
to hide your torso from neighbour eyes while maggoty mind control
made me feel like I was losing all control over my own body; I smelled
a brief dose of silly wild flowers in between the air was neither hot
nor cold you'll never pull this off just to set the scene for your seventeen
year old melodrama power trip pool perverted abuse express not off
Broadway at all, this street still runs from Serena Gundy all the way
to Yonge, in the city of Toronto, the city of our youth where
our skeletons still phantom in deleted energy outlines on the curbs
where our sneakers would rest, in front of the houses who hid everything
but their opulent garbage and here we lay amongst the menace of soiled
hampers rotten in the state our hour is almost come, when we to sulph'rous
and tormenting flames ousted at last so art thou to a most mystical revenge

DAVID LEE ROTH CHARLES BUKOWSKI FREE REFILLS

for Kathy Acker

Women need to become literary "criminals,"
break the literary laws and reinvent their own,
because
the established laws prevent women from presenting
the reality of their lives
even a woman who has the soul of a pirate,
at least pirate morals, even a woman who prefers
loneliness to the bickerings and constraints
of heterosexual marriage, even such a woman
who is a freak in our society needs a home

the only characteristic freaks share
is our knowledge that we don't
fit in
the only reaction against an unbearable society
is equally unbearable nonsense

PARKLIFE

He believes in verdict: the indulgence
is confident, brilliant, makes him alive.
The hurt is a well-tailored welt he'll keep
in mint condition; a conversation preference
a piece of talk, healing
without proper ointment,
always in stitches, his body a mute
variable, auctioned off to his own hysterics.
Timeless we fall, setting off
and setting up, the you-bomb ticking...
The cartilage, the infinite flash of domestic
potential, of social pairing, of juvenile kite strings
tearing the clouds, tearing at every cloud.

He wakes up, miles from the cinders,
the pyrotechnics and glucose-wash-tongue spit
drying on wilted municipal flowers
not an apparition, something deliberate
eventually cruel; not a conclusion drawn
from some tinsel-drunk napkin sketch Cinderella
hopped up on disenchanting materials
with subjective scorn, villain here has
milked this anthem, jingle and all, rendering
love pitiless for all occasions
until the tattoo eclipses the skin

O how he will be fine, colliding in
blue silence by the chandelier's sour glow
soldering tears of resolve face, a thick tide
as heart drowns in present tense, tightens:
please don't worry or feel
guilty or whatever is going
through your head
let the projections melt
if they leave a sticky residue
on your fingers
don't run your hands
through your hair

'SILVERBLADE' NOVELIST MARGARET ATWOOD

is not thinking about the snowman poem I accused
her of writing back in 2008[2], she is thinking of a toothless
man sobbing maudlin in a dirty sweat sock...no, now
it's a goofy flower man, an immigrant, no, a seventh
generation landed immigrant from London, no a goofy
flower man who is part wolf and part praying mantis
in need of money needing it badly for his expanding
family, and he is so tired the toothless man,
who we remember to be sobbing in a dirty sweat sock,
seems to be back in contention you see, Margaret Atwood
is brainstorming, thunder makes her wonder
about her new antagonist, a monster father, chief
abandoner of girls and boys he sires, toothless in head
and heart, no longer bothering to sell flowers, he is a man sobbing
loudly into a dirty sweat sock who just wanted to sell
his plasma to pay to have his eyebrows darkened
a highly sought after feature by employers looking to employ
the upper crust, it's an elaborate procedure done in Akron, Ohio
the first procedure took place in 2383 he is sobbing, this false
father character sketch, I saw the sawdust under my own father's
work table watching the blade's slowing spins and each tooth,
canine and perfect, left no trace of its harsh chew

---

[2]On Twitter @MargaretAtwood and I had an exchange, she even offered, ever my mother, to look for it in her office when she got home. You can ask her about it, I doubt she'll remember me, but are you saying that poetry is non-fiction? #truestory #Atwood #nolie

SULPICIA'S SCHOOL FOR BAD GIRLS

GEMINUS VEXILLUM

Sulpicia puella docta "learned girl"
an elegist more than a cultivated mistress,
more than a cultural it girl so gifted with

song yet her poems were left for
dead by dead men of letters thousands

of years from one sunny
Ancient Roman day in which she wrote
softly, wrote hardly, wrote

six surviving elegies and then and then
the men these men them men
who decide things in the 20th century

found them condemned by gender
to a century and a half of condes-
cension disregard and willful misconstruction

to accommodate the inelastic
politics of elderly male philologists
other men felt awful things

lacking any display of erudition
in no way academic "amateur" "artless"
"simply a pastiche constructed from

what she has read" don't forget
how she "shows little sign
or awareness of other poets"

"personal and non-universalised"
she witnessed her loneliness
after her third drink; until then

she gently ginwronged the crowd,
on these abashed ash streets, piers,
peep shows pulled at her heart carry-

ing her heart sneer along the front,
the badge of loneliness bleated
beating under white sun, life held vitriol

nothing warned her: I'll spoil your looks
it spoke to her in the music, she only
felt her grayscale loneliness

as time travelling abuse husbands
raking in academic fever
whiplash horseshit lame?

chaste matronae, ideally identified bodies
rejecting moral code bound up
in those gold clothes

here lies a worthy spy, Sappho says
   in the stuffy houses of men
I'm scarred, beyond my grief

thanks a lot, Tibullus for these
humane remains a poet without
a book, no heart no face no spine

we rolled onto the fuss

   even I can say—I'm
better off
   on my rich pillow my

clean hair the night shakes
against faithful mountainous
home is where the heart

is most fragrant
how can you call
this place anything

but homely?
I'm all the rage
You enrage me

cease engagement
rake down your boneless back
never revealing your true hide

while I trickle stars into my mouth
for sustenance, oh look here
comes my luminous friends

real in form I hear elegant
Emily Hauser from
Yale University who speaks

as she refreshes her drink:

"Taking a recently identified elegiac poem of Sulpicia,
a graffito written by a Pompeiian tibicina, and the verse
cento of Proba in turn, I look at how female authors
attempted to articulate identity as women and as authors
both within and at the margins of the dominant male literary
tradition, and how vocabulary responds to (and often
subverts) the terminology deployed by male authors"

we smoke like literate bad-lunged leather
undergrads stress coma patience

charcoal grey slashing our hazel eyes
we discuss probiotics, old erotica

take me away; throw me heart elsewhere
as rude Rome makes the lilac rules

I don't want a jackass teacher[3] kicking me
soundly off my brutal library chair

---

[3]My daughter had a teacher in grade four who pulled her chair out from under her—only to later deny it. The incident happened when no one was in the classroom save for teacher and student. Three months of meetings and my child was told it never happened. One of the other teachers who lied about the incident got a promotion. To this day my daughter has had to live with the memory of a room full of grown-ups convincing her she was not telling the truth. But as Leonard Cohen once said, "Poetry is a verdict".

SULPICIA'S ROMAN GRANDMOTHER

Poultice clouds came crashing down my love
in the shape of romance – a phantom esoteric

curling my heart with puns and daggers, we spoke
back then in a messy southpaw grammar, battling

young corporeal mechanics, butting heads
conquers insomnia's bursary on an evening

of time spending our feet over fences thousands
of minutes ago when life was thinner thousands

of days ago sweaty palms, night classes hot seats
wine glasses tongue in mouth can you still see them

stars oh dear self, up there, so much older? The ones
which hung so well when our shadows beckoned, when I,

Sulpicia chirped one of my grandma's broken Roman
songs so lovely in the honey fed mornings of death

KATHY ACKER RIDES THE BUS

To her, every road wasn't made of material itself
but animalistic memory and sensory sent out

the way bats see, bouncing infrared animation
depicting what we can't recognize or the way

other worlds contact us, as if we are riding over
people's dreams, dog's dreams, made of ancestral

bones made of skin clouds made of a million
cravings, bank robbing sister's shameful tears

I didn't create language, Kathy thought. It was hell
in high school, guts busted, noses bleeding. Later

she would think about her mother and father
the people she loved. Now she wants to tell us

teenaged smartypants that the world is a complicated
place you can put ribbons on everything but it doesn't

change the fact that beauty isn't something
you can pluck from a grocery hearse I mean

everyone is different and feels

fucked up for no reason but there is always
a fucking reason

SULPICIA'S BREAKFAST FEEDBACK

Miss "Maybe I'm a masochist" stands barefoot talcum snow
outlined toes in a blouse the colour of flour in a frenzy she
moves with scorpion grace carrying the candelabra towards
the large Picasso to get a closer look at five nude females
in various stages of business in a house the colour of lead

Sulpicia bows her heavy head, moves the guests towards
the porch to feed each a poached egg, toast and cranberry juice
now get a closer look at five nude females this morning, in
various digestive states

JUNKYARD BEACH HOME

You must have musta mustard robbed a junkyard
to get a face like that throw him through throw him
from the bridge wise friend into the night's earth
by the warlocks' toothy smile outlaw clouds line
your consciousness bright forth the mighty ghost
yesterday and today how many days and more your
eyes taught me to count slow in self-imposed summer
drought until one afternoon bright and green eyeing
muscular legs, you want to eat evening breasts buoyant
in the bottle-green sea don't get all nuts relive the rejection
of foul play of rooster pecks last I heard you were filing
a wrongful birth suit against your parents and the province
of New Brunswick his face was eager and I lied to him
about finding a bowling pin in a human body so impossible
to mend, knock over again while the north wind
that parts our hair see how nature collides and wacks us
suo marte = *in mutual slaughter*

CONSTRICTOR

We were not the richest family
in Leaside, we were in the bottom
rung of earners—my part-time
paper route plus my father's
income from the insurance
business (heavily taxed at the
tobacco stands) he worked hard
was withdrawn to whatever
hobbies gardening solitaire coin
collecting quiet couch coffee sips
newspapers read, delivered to the
home where we lived: a modest
two-story that had been converted
from a bungalow the scotch tape
along the ceiling still visible from
the upgrade until dad just painted
over it and hoped the tape would
stick while the broadloom was
installed upside down with a toxic
glue—unfriendly nails jutted out
deliberately tip out, the shank
gleaming like the tiniest metal
weed you ever did see in the
hallway, the head buried beneath
the bristly underside "We
borrowed the glue from the
church" Mom cackled while Dad
laughed "It's the same glue that
helped repair the crucifix which
hangs behind the spooky Dracula
organ" our second floor was
sparse with two bedrooms and a
miniscule bathroom that boasted a
double sink a mirror a toilet a door
I lived in the converted rec room
in our basement painted blue

drowning came naturally we rarely
went on vacation or entertained
our grandparents and uncles would
visit on holidays my friends were
my only escape from the tense
mood I can't remember if I met
Andrew at Northlea United
Church or Northlea Public School
in March 1981 and I was in the
first grade we had just moved
from Mount Pleasant and Eglinton
to Laird Eglinton essentially a few
kilometres but to me it was more
than just a new house—*I was
saying goodbye* to a retinue of
friends I'd be matriculating with at
Maurice Coady since 1978 they
had names like Darby, Eric,
Jonathan, Brian, Sandy, Josh,
Kevin, Peter, and Amy, March
break hit and when I returned I
was the new kid trying to
remember everyone's name: Kara,
Ara, Sarah, Joanna, Myles, Todd,
John, Christopher, James and
Andrew while my lunch was
always ruined with eel bites! while
carcinogenic tears hung enormous
really and if I could say anything
to Northlea Public school it would
be this: you still have the same
postal code, smell like the same
piece of chicken and listen to
music made in the 1600s during
school dances so quit telling me to
get on with my life I've moved 65

times since 1996 I've had 19 different phone numbers 39 different roommates lived in four different provinces breeding a certain longing for calm I was starting the first grade all over again with a classroom of brand-new peers with slightly better haircuts who could spell Wayne Gretzky and Jari Kurri and Mike Palmateer and Guy Lafleur my physicality began to bother me shortest male in my class and Mrs Olsen had a height chart for all to see like a mug shot line up minus two-way glass Myles and Andrew were the tallest and I was below, far below Nathaniel in a deep blue marker with all the short girls swimming in vertical obscurity seemed to be the only currency I still carry with me sometimes I can see myself from outside myself in the memory like this: I am 5 years old in Newton Massachusetts walking across the top aisle of a drugstore with my father he's kind of there but not there. As I am walking, I look down the aisle to my left and across the bisecting aisle, on the corner facing me—unmistakable beaconing franchise logo in black and silver with the iconic words at the top in such a way as it always was. It was a display stand in full of *Star Wars* figurines I don't want to sound glib but it was as though I was directed there by a divine force. The talented marketing team at Kenner had prepared me well for this moment a moment I felt it in my stomach and my face flushed and my ears rang and now when I see myself from the perspective of the figurine stand and I zoom in on my utter amazement the memory is fading a bit and I can't remember what figures were there not a large variety I seem to remember the Death Squad Commander exciting and erotic, I can almost smell the fumes from the fresh plastic and card stock packaging swaddling those beauties this memory remains it signifies the first time I remember *REALLY* wanting something with a terrible keening desire. And this, I think, was before I even saw the movie! I wanted to meld myself with *Star Wars*. I would have eaten *Star Wars* if I could. It was the first time I remember fetishizing something and the dynamic has repeated itself over and over in my life but never again with the same magical intensity as that day it thrust me with a great deal of influence on the symbolic order of my young

mind, shepherding me
I remember regularly dreaming
about being in a particular
submerged mall in Halifax that
was populated by the lesser
characters of the galaxy universe
and when I was quite young I
would conflate my reality and the
space opera in a variety of ways I
was years from the psyche babble
Sunnybrook Hospital past the
soccer field where heavy lungs
legs deep in green knit socks like
most children and other ego
maniacs I had a suspicion that I
was the star of a movie that was in
constant production featuring,
amongst other icons (Big Bird,
Ernie and Bert) Luke, Han and C-
3Po. I remember peeing in our
downstairs bathroom one day and
struggling with the fact that being
in this fantasy meant that Leia
could watch me pee until my
stomach trembled homesick,
feeling weird in an underwater
dream mall in Halifax, a city I had
never been to, even the bleached
foods from the era nourished all of
us waspy in synthetic orgies of
saran wrap, carbonated lemonade,
relished the silent auction of life,
living in ultimate time-bomb
surrender never exchanging harsh
words, soothing me from the real
world, my relentless at six anger

when I cut my hand on our glass
door and my friend said to me
how I would forever have less
blood than he had, how I'd never
catch up to him as I washed in the
bathroom, the blood down the
drain and my paling face in the
mirror I've bled since, however I
have no accurate number and no
longer have contact with Brian,
whose glass door cut me open and
stunted my spiritual growth on any
given Saturday. There were bike
rides on Rumsey on Hanna on
Beaufield where I escaped this
dirty world where I blurred by on
Saturdays uncalm and itchy
Sunday mornings at Northlea
United Church where I met
Andrew whose family worked in
the funeral business and were
upper-middle class with an
opulent home dark brown stained
banisters new blue tiles in the
kitchen floor, a fireplace living
room with a sliding glass door to
the backyard to spread out to play
I would see him across the pews at
Northlea United Church in our
strange religious clothing where I
auditioned for Kid in Church #4
(petulant little shit disturber in the
making, a bottom rung entitled
white kid from a so-so greedy
neighbourhood only interested in
self-guided passions such as

hockey, bimbo teen VHS rentals
to get my required lust
supplements, and not at all
interested in the prehistoric
ramblings of organ swapping
religious characters peeing their
pants with worry about damnation
and crops turning to dust). No one
farmed in Leaside anymore, and
so, an hour later after Sunday
school was out Andrew and I
made friendship plans over juice
and cookies a bike ride in the park
a firecracker in our palms our
families knew each other didn't
socialize when it came out in
theatres that June Andrew's father
took us to see *Blade Runner* at
seeing the large Pepsi sign by the
snacking area its Americana
colour wheel I screamed out my
joy for the soft drink, the electric
caloric product its fountainousness
reminded me I was not at home
but my enthusiasm bought me a
look from Andrew's father as if I
wasn't being polite enough in my
hysterical excitement about
everything around me "I WANT
A PEPSI!" Andrew's father
looked at me like I was being rude
and said something along the lines
of *we'll see* I felt ashamed for my
desire, an eight-year-old *don't be
greedy* but I got the Pepsi and
some popcorn and I said thank you

for Andrew and I were friends for all seasons: tobogganing in Serena Gundy park trips to his cottage go-kart rides and even trips to the Granite Club in North York for the occasional fancy hamburger. When I left Northlea to take French Immersion at Cosburn Middle School I saw more of Andrew on the bus because he went to a special program at a different school for the rich and mediocre bus transfers wrapped around our fingers like papier-mâché one October evening (the thirtieth, a Friday, I didn't go to the school dance, I was afraid, I couldn't dance! I told Andrew, and he put on Doin' the Pigeon to cheer me up, an impromptu anti-reality dance lesson, as if I would dance that way in public!) This was after the market crashed after Black Monday and that evening the phone kept ringing because we were calling or I was calling girls I knew and we played *California Games* on his Commodore 64 "Nate's only going out with her to get popular" Andrew told a girl named Sarah on the phone I was only going out with a girl named Corey at school to be popular he told someone that on the phone the gossip got to Corey and I was dumped on Monday at school

Andrew was my friend though he
looked that way—a friend of
mine—he had hair eyes teeth
language memory and strength he
had a hockey stick a bike a wallet
blue eyes dirty blonde hair
somewhat shaggy he laughed
loudly he ate Mr. Sub his dad
brought me one a few times too—
but he shouldn't have spread that
rumour that wasn't even true—
about Corey it didn't seem to
bother me though, not for very
long, maybe a lunch hour or two, a
few dozen spins of *New Order* I
was pretty shy back then I knew I
was attracted to girls and love as
the early evening shade began its
slowburn didn't seem to bother
my sense of fate for very long, I
was pretty shy back then and now
the waitress taketh and the
waitress giveth and now I'm a sad
fucker with a cruel burnt stub for a
penis. *Didn't you force me to suck*
your cock a few times rich boy? as
bitchy payment to be your friend?
Now look at me. But were it late
1987 the phone would be a
ranging after the malicious dinner
hour then all the hours *Sarah Tara*
Holly Brenda Fiona Sarah again
and again the cute denim Cotton
Ginny girl list of grade sevens
lilting their lipgloss tones into my
cuteboy landline ear, girls who

dug my carefree bad grade getting
grade eight ways until one near
summer life seemed to overflow
one near summer the weather
made my bed cold each night right
at dinner much to the chagrin of
my mother who didn't want my
fish sticks to get cold she wanted
high choreography low
carbohydrates never used butter
one summer one near summer one
near summertalking to them on the
phone at all hours *Sarah Tara*
Holly Brenda who dug my
carefree bad grade getting grade
eight ways seemed to overflow
each night right at dinner much to
the chagrin of my mother who
didn't want my fish sticks and
carrot to get cold she wanted high
choreography low carbohydrates
and never used butter. One
summer Andrew and I wore
matching outfits movies shopping
swimming bike rides all those
gateway joys of the nineteen
eighties my psyche my favourite
heroes from this era always bring
with them a layer of invisible
sadness for could I really watch
the late eighties heroes wrestle the
bad guys without his ghost
bothering me, fiddling with me
could I hear a late eighties pop
song of substance of faith and
high-hat without being transported

to Andrew's den? I detailed my friendship's growth with God: but God didn't mind the sexual abuse I guess so Andrew continued while I pinballed around the affluent family home a family of blonde children sitcom like in their glamour perfection I was drawn to them so different from the brown haired brown eyed nutrition waifs I lived with a friend remarked to me, after seeing photos of my brother and I at 4 and eight "you look so delicate" as if we were made of Fun Dip dust and paper one September evening Andrew's father bought his eldest son the vinyl single "I Want Your Sex" a new song about sex while his bikini body sister teased us about the song or so Andrew would point out—my sister is in her bathing suit, check it out his older bro was a tall cricket of a man at nearly six five while Andrew the middle child had a bit of baby fat still lingering on his six two frame one afternoon in grade nine I came home with a floppy disk Andrew had let me use for an assignment when I went to open the list of files on my trusty second hand Commodore 64 I accidentally opened one called My Mother's Death his older brother

had written for school and in it
was a first person account
detailing the day they came home
to find their mother unconscious
on the kitchen floor—a floor I had
traversed across countless times I
read with true crime intrigue about
her brain aneurysm I never asked
why Andrew had no mother—it
was clear his primary caregiver
was his father and he'd also have
someone at home a housekeeper
who would cook him a hot meal
when his dad had to work late I
never knew what happened to his
mother up until this point—I'm
sure his mother's death when he
was five or six hurt Andrew more
than I'd ever know I can't imagine
where I'd have wound up in 1981
had my mother dropped dead on
our greasy kitchen floor. My
father certainly couldn't have
raised us alone my brother and I
would have likely been shipped
off to an aunt's house until things
could get stabilized while living
together my parents' lives were
never hidden or exaggerated we
all knew within the hour what was
on the agenda: a few minutes on
how much money was saved
switching to pork from chicken
from beef week to week meal to
meal the cat played crazily with
empty plastic bags every Saturday

at noon when our blue Buick
grocery hearse brought the bright
red maggot meat from the 656
Eglinton Avenue Dominion and
for a while my mother loved my
younger brother better because he
was less embarrassing and a while
turned into forever but she showed
me the paperwork I almost saw
her point when I first went to the
dentist they laughed her out of the
white tooth of a room with my
rotten baby teeth in her hands
"You can't feed a nineteen
seventy-four baby orange juice all
day woman!" Let's set the scene
for I am running out of time its
mid-morning September Sixth
Nineteen Eighty-Eight I have
white converse even after Labour
Day 100 days since the yearbook
ink and my grade nine spine is
broken—looking back one grade
to the future it doesn't hurt, plus I
can hear the cheers on a day off I
return to visit the new grade eights
now crown queens + kings who
walk backwards in time; a familiar
infinity someone recognizes me as
I cross the field. I can hear I hear I
heard the cheers as sets of
beautiful friendhands slammed
passionate against the window
panes a crowded second or two to
add to my highlight reel of
subjective fame my feet keep in

time, left, right, left, right—I'm
taking my time basking in the
Greek restaurant where we all eat
fries we are all more thoroughbred
than clotheshorses—the new
addition size seven and a half, my
white Chucks back to school new
(converse first day of school shoes
flooded the feet of all cool callow
preteens in North American
matriculation culture) returned me
to paradise middle before
returning to Leaside and my high
school cage, thinking, I've still got
it...little did I know how little I
knew the warm bleak cruel and
true, quietly seeding several
acerbic morning clouds full of
concrete sadness soon to sandbag
me before the post-sacred era
before it all smashed and ruined
society and we were all allowed to
be free without statements of
intent, we were all silly sweet
lambs, silent and free while the
banshee sings with bits of blurry
Kodak paper showing along the
gums bits of me in my sexual teen
hockey outfits—garters and all the
cotton fuzz cover bits the banshee
has eaten my subjective
memorabilia my matter Kodak
hours reproducing dramatic
gestures of intolerance in a Texas
episode of pleated pants of
saturated hair and make up

entrepreneurial television in which
the central plot is an oil-greed
family liquor liver types opening
actor credit slap symphony lovely
helicopter footage cityscape green
from the football Cowboy's home
turf plaid shirts mistresses eating
juicy pears in negligee belt
buckles thrown up into ceiling
fans, herds of steer run off the
screen as Nielsen talks numbers as
our family gets high "Did all that
really happen to you?" whatever
catharsis I was banking on didn't
materialize and I kept on dragging
my abusive chains with me as I
began to raise my daughter with
my wife I would continue to have
outbursts every couple of months
overreactions to things that most
normal men wouldn't even raise
an eyebrow about I couldn't shake
the dirty feeling the anger that had
been seeded in me one warm
evening in August 1988 when I
thought my best friend had my
best intentions in mind no one
would find out if they did it would
be easy to dismiss me as mentally
ill, PSYCHO NATE is what they
called me mid-1990s when Drew
Barrymore went bi-polar on the
big screen with the guy who
played Robin maybe my mother
told someone at church that I was
in and out of hospitals stigma

stuck nicely as did any erratic behaviour. Dealing with our own past traumas in modern times, like most North Americans my wife and I binge watch shows about kidnappings rapists and serial killers which got me thinking about just how long I had been exposed to hearing about other people's sexual abuse the way the victims always women would describe their attackers always depressed me when it came to the Golden State Killer I was so frustrated at how the villain had evaded capture for decades and got to live out a normal life while his victims relived his torture on a daily basis. He must have found comfort in those endless days on end until his arrest with my therapist with whom I meet each month virtually (we have only met once or twice in real life) I've been able to negotiate an understanding of what happened to me as a teenager but inside my adult mind what seemed blatantly obvious perhaps to others wasn't obvious to me at all. It took a Yoda-like speech from a friend over the summer who tragically took his own life a month later for me to realise that what Andrew wanted with me was to have power to lord over someone who was both physically too small to defend himself but also who desperately needed a friend. This was the guy who came to my house with a bat an hour after the police told my father to cool off at his parents' place in Kingston for christ's sake he was my hero but what happened to him to make him behave this way towards me? I remember a couple of instances with his older and even taller brother would become physical with and overpower Andrew which was no small feat one instance in particular always stood out: we were listening to George Michael's lounge singer styled ballad "Kissing A Fool" on vinyl in the living room when his brother began to sit on Andrew's lap, and sat there for the entire song Andrew was powerless in his older brother's lock and in true older brother fashion—was hamming it up and really getting his little brother's goat as George sang he would sing into Andrew's ear, pretending to be a sleazy lounge singer making the moves on Andrew who was yelling squirming trying his best to escape. Was this something that happened regularly? Was Andrew's perverse grooming of me a compensation for his own

sense of raging powerlessness
in a family of blonde giants?
"Nathaniel it's not your secret"
my therapist reminds me "It's *his*
secret" My agent asked me how I
thought Andrew would react if I
told this story publicly I didn't
answer him because it was both
impossible to answer but also
depressing to fantasize about an
answer that would in any way
make my claims seem invalid
what Andrew did to me under the
nose of his family how he got rid
of me as a friend and how one
time I told him I thought he was
disgusting and I didn't want to do
this anymore, I would begin to
prepare for decades of social
anxieties self-harm and the
absolute fear of being judged by
my own family who historically
have never really been that
empathetic of my struggles. So I
told his family one night not too
long ago I called up Andrew's
father a woman answered the
phone I asked to speak him by
name saying I was from Northlea
United Church. When he
answered I asked him if he was
the father of Andrew's older brother
and Andrew I asked him if
he remembered Nate from Leaside
he said he did "I just wanted to
speak to you because I wanted you

to know that from August 1988
until the spring of 1992 your son
Andrew sexually abused me."
Likely still rotund, he hung up the
phone I stood in my frozen
driveway in tears shouting
"You're hanging up on me"?
I walked to my wife's office "I
called him I called Andrew's dad
and told him" I made one more
call that evening to Andrew's
older brother and got his machine
I politely left a message of similar
trivia, the hardest part of all was
coming, tears were now replaced
by gasping cries as I dialed my
father's phone number we hadn't
spoken for several years "Are you
going to hang up on me?" I
demanded to know "Look Dad
I know that I haven't been the
greatest son I know you're turning
eighty this year I just I have to tell
you something." And so I did. The
connection wasn't that good and
we agreed to speak later I heard
love in his voice that I thought he
was no longer capable of I
regretted our bouts of silence he
said a short prayer-like fragment
to me and I told him I loved him
my wife joined me outside where I
was now howling into the night's
sky "He loves me!" I cried "My
dad loves me!" I called my mother
and got her boyfriend Bill "Are

you alone mom" I asked her "I need you to go somewhere alone" I couldn't hear her response because I told her after I tell you this you can't say anything and I am getting off the phone. My wife and I went for a walk with her clutching my torso with all her might our bodies connecting as best they could in the cold "I'm so proud of you" she kept saying. That night I slept like a baby. In the morning I didn't feel like a two hundred and fifteen pound forty-six year old I felt younger and lighter I was on a path now towards something true something real I felt empowered I felt less angry and this is just the beginning of a freedom that I have been unable to touch for nearly thirty years. The last time I ever saw Andrew was in February 1994 working as a pallbearer for some extra cash during my first year of university I didn't realise what funeral home it would be at since my father was working for a few different companies at the time after being fired in late-1990 that is a lie I knew full well which funeral home I would be working at what I didn't know was they were short-staffed and Andrew was filling in too I remember that I had just dyed my hair purple and

had to drive to Shoppers Drug
Mart to get some dye to make
myself presentable my father and I
drove to the funeral home and
were greeted by the funeral
director and the other pallbearers.
Andrew was one of them. He
looked at my father and myself
and in a lowly voice said "What
the hell?" We didn't speak
through the entire service silent
the black gloved drive back
together I asked to be let off at
Laird and Eglinton the corner
where Andrew and I grew up on
sugary snacks in between bike
rides and toboggan runs three
weeks later my dad handed me a
cheque for seventy-five dollars I
looked at it for a few weeks before
cashing it the surreal object and its
officious coldness bothered me
here was money made out to me
from the bank account of a family
who were both putting food on our
table and simultaneously
undermining my self-esteem I
eventually cashed the cheque and
never saw Andrew again.

NOTES

The title of this book is taken from the Sears BMX Constrictor I bought with my own money in the early 1980s, which kept me in and out of trouble and allowed me to come and go...

"David Lee Roth Charles Bukowski Free Refills:"

I wrote the title of this poem and this sentence
but Kathy Acker wrote the rest. I am also responsible
for the line
breaks.

If you know someone who is being sexually abused, please reach out and offer help in any way. If you are being sexually abused, please talk to your doctor, your parents, an aunt or uncle. Don't go through this alone.

ACKNOWLEDGEMENTS

Thank you Denis and Mansfield for believing in me once more.

Thanks to Jim Johnstone once more in 2021, for editing graciously and with care. We'll always have *Thermos*.

Thanks to Jean Marc Ah-Sen, rob mclennan and Sonia Di Placido for their support and sharing their art with all of us.

Thanks to Warren, my bandmate in Proper Concern who had a hand in the rhythm of this album, I mean, book's title track. And to my nineties friends, the friends that saved my life: Dragan, Kerry Holly, Tavis, Caroline, Lesley, Neil and Carey and the memory of Katie Lameck who left us too soon in 2015. "Frogmen, 1995" was based on a memory of being in London, Ontario with my friend Katie and hearing about teenagers lost on Lake Ontario. Katie, you were one of my first real friends.

Thanks to Spencer Gordon, my little brother in the ring and in impossible art.

Nathaniel G. Moore is the author of three novels and four poetry collections, a book of essays (*Honorarium*) and numerous articles and reviews which have appeared in print across Canada. Born in Toronto in 1974, he lives now in Fredericton with his wife, writer Amber McMillan, and their child, and runs moorehype, his boutique publishing publicity firm.